You Are a
Masterpiece!

Seeing Yourself as God Sees You

BUMMI NIYONU ANDERSON

Published by:
Double Xposure Media Group

Published by Double Xposure Media Group
Renaissance Connection, LLC
323 Pine Avenue Suite 205
Albany, GA 31701

Scripture taken from the New King James Version®. Copyright © 1982 by Thomas Nelson, Inc. Used by permission. All rights reserved.

Cover design and photography by Femi N. Anderson
Manuscript Editing by Cecily Pouncil & Linda Brown
Make up by Judith M. Corbett

Copyright © 2011 Bummi Niyonu Anderson. This book or parts thereof may not be reproduced in any form, stored in a retrieval system, or transmitted in any form by any means- electronic, mechanical, photocopy, recording, or otherwise- without prior written permission of the publisher, except as provided by United States of America copyright law.

ISBN: 0615524710

ISBN-13: 978-0615524719

DEDICATION

for those who are beautiful
those who are special
all who struggle to know it

I will praise You, for I am fearfully and wonderfully made; marvelous are Your works. And that my soul knows very well

Psalm 139:14

CONTENTS

	Introduction	9
1	First Things First	11
2	Image is Everything	15
3	Mirror Mirror On the Wall	19
4	Identity Crisis 101	23
5	Another Man's Treasure	27
6	You Are a Masterpiece!	30
7	Poetry in Motion	34
8	When God Made You	37
9	Beloved of God	41
10	The Gift of You	47
11	The Heir Apparent	52
12	In the Hands of the Potter	55
13	Sticks and Stones	58
14	The Mind of God	62
15	You're No Ugly Duckling!	65
16	And Peter	68

17	Walk on Water!	73
18	Lights! Camera! Action!	77
19	A Friend of God	81
20	Fear Not!	86
21	Epilogue: A Learned Behavior	90
22	TOOLS	94
23	Hard Questions Hard Answers	97
	About the Author	
	Order Information	

INTRODUCTION

For a long time, my own self worth and beauty was an ongoing struggle for me. My struggle was exacerbated one day when a college professor who had never met my twin sister crushed what little self esteem I had. Being a twin had always been the highlight of my life, so when the opportunity came to introduce Femi to someone that had only heard of her, I leaped at the chance. I saw this professor from afar and called out to her, "Dr.____ I want you to meet my twin sister!" As we approached her, she looked at the both of us and said, "Let me see who is the prettiest." It was a contest I knew I was not going to win. It was a microcosm of what I had felt throughout my life. Femi and I have always been as different as day and night, and our differences measured themselves in a lot of ways, including skin complexion. People always saw her as the prettier one because she was light-skinned and I brown-skinned. We were, in my opinion, the epitome of the color complex in the African-American community: the lighter-skinned African-American always seemed to be viewed as better than and/or treated better than the darker-skinned African-American. In some ways that complexity seeped over into how I saw myself. I had grown up believing that black was beautiful, but for me, at times, it was a social observation alone. It would be many years later before I would be comfortable in my own skin and all comparisons did not matter. Just as I had been overlooked by that professor years ago, one day a friend said to me, "You have the prettiest eyes I've ever seen!" Really? I had never taken the time to look, blinded by my own insecurities. After hearing this, I stood in front of my mirror. I took my glasses off and stared at myself for several minutes. Most of my life had been spent thinking I did not measure up; I had failed to notice all the things that made me beautiful. This one encounter alone radically changed me. God, in His wisdom, used my friend's observation to help change how I saw myself. I no longer stand in the mirror and repeat to myself my own disdain. Through getting to know God and in turn, Him telling me who I was, I have spent the last 14 years standing in front of the mirror acknowledging my own beauty and declaring my own worth.

In writing this book, I wanted to share with others what I believe God has shared with me. The greatest revelation, beyond a personal relationship with God, is seeing ourselves as God sees us. You would be surprised to know He sees us for who we are. He has no pretensions about us. He has counted us valuable and wonderful.

Seeing yourself as God sees you can be quite a journey. The journey for me, though at times painfully reflective, has been worth the reward. I pray you find the same.

1
FIRST THINGS FIRST
God Sees You as the Person He Wants to Know

You will never come to any place of significance without God. In reality, that is really what the search is all about. All the emptiness we feel is because we try to fill the voids in our lives with people or things. Both lack the ability to fill us. There are places in our lives only God is meant to occupy and to attempt to let other things occupy those places is superficial. I can remember when all I felt I needed to exist was the love of another woman. My sense of longing led to deep hurt. Many of us spend our lives on a quest to find that one person, place, or thing that will answer all of our questions. The issues of life gnaw at us, so we look everywhere for validation, but rarely to the only true Validator. He made us. He knows all about us. It is His stamp of approval we so desperately need, yet seldom seek. We search every nook and cranny for the love and affection of other people, but God wants us to search and need Him to the same degree, if not more. The Apostle Paul said it best when he proclaimed, "For in Him we live, move, and have our being" (Acts 17:28). I ask the question: do you live, move, and exist in God or have you, like me, spent most of your life looking for love in all the wrong places? All of us, at some point or another, come to a crossroad in life where we are faced with indecision and challenges. It is often at this place we are invited to meet God, to go back to the very beginning of our own existence.

There is a woman in the Bible (John 4:3-26) who is often referred to as *the Samaritan Woman*. She is like many of us. I am sure she had no idea when she left home that morning to get water from Jacob's well, that she was going to meet God. How many of us have had that experience? We did not know we were about to meet God, but guess what, God knew. That is why He made it His business to be there when she got there. In fact, Jesus said He *needed* to go to Samaria. He needed to go meet a woman who had spent most of her life longing to be loved and accepted. Her search was evident because she had been married five times and was living with a man when she encountered Jesus. Jesus knew her entire history. He knew what kind of life she had led and He knew of her longing. I believe what He was really saying by being at the right place at the right time was, "I know you because I created you, so I know what you need. I am what you have been looking for." I believe the Samaritan woman had spent all those years trying to fill a void in her life that only God could fill. There are places in our lives that only God can fill and I do not care how much you look to someone else, that place will always be void.

Another lesson that can be gleaned from the Samaritan woman's story is that when she encountered Jesus she felt inadequate. She asked Him knowing the culture, why He, a Jew, was even talking to her, a Samaritan woman. She knew Jews did not interact with Samaritans. How many times have you asked yourself, "Who am I?" This is what she was implying about herself. Even though she did not know it was God at the time of the initial encounter, she could no doubt avoid her own feelings of unworthiness. It was the love of God that drew her to her divine appointment. It is that same love that draws you to Him. Yes, you may feel as if you do not deserve His love and rightfully so, but He wants to give it to you anyway. He broke culture and tradition to offer Himself to her, and that is what He will do for you. He is as desperate for a relationship with you as you are desperate for all the things you feel you need. I always say God is the biggest addict because He is so addicted to us. He emphatically cannot get enough of His creation! Even in your worst state, God sees your best. Believe me, God is head over heels in love with you and when you are not with Him, He is love sick. If you are ready to accept that everything starts with a personal relationship with God through Jesus Christ, pray this prayer:

Father, in the name of Jesus, I know You know all things. Before I was born, You knew me and You had plans for my life. Father, I thank You, that I am Your best creation and I accept a relationship with You. I acknowledge I am a sinner and ask You to forgive me of my sins. Father, I confess that You gave your Son Jesus Christ for my sins and that He died on the Cross. I confess that Jesus Christ is Lord. Father, thank You for saving me. Father, I ask that You reveal your plans for my life. In the name of Jesus, I pray. Amen.

2
IMAGE IS EVERYTHING
God Sees You as His Child

It is very important that we learn to see ourselves as God sees us. Our God-view of ourselves is often contrary to what we have been led to believe. First, it is paramount that we view God correctly. He is not sitting on His throne in heaven with a humongous baseball bat waiting to whack us over the head with it. He is not waiting for us to mess up so He can punish us nor is he lurking over our mistakes like Freddie Kruger. No, if anything His arms are outstretched wide to receive us, and to love us like we have never been loved before. He wants to hug us, not hang us. Sadly enough too many Christians have this all too awkward image of God. There are those who call themselves believers who actually believe God is simply waiting to get them or pay them back for something. I agree that there can be consequences to some of our actions, but God is not void of compassion and love for us. He does not want to be viewed as a hostile, uncompassionate God. He wants to be our Father. Seeing God as your Father might be difficult to comprehend if the image of your biological father is tarnished, especially if you never knew your father or he was emotionally disconnected from you.

I have some very distinct memories of my daddy, Ed Anderson. When we were growing up, all the kids in the neighborhood were afraid of him, and understandably so. He was tall (6'0), big, and had an afro, so the kids tried their best to avoid him. I guess you could say he had everybody's respect. Even when there were disputes between our neighbors across the street from us, he refused to take sides because he could not testify to something he did not witness firsthand. I can remember one occasion that my father disciplined me. It is forever etched in my memory.

My twin sister and I walked to and from school the first three years of our elementary education. My mother, Willa, worked for an organization that required her to do a lot of traveling so she was away often. One particular morning, our father drove us to school because it was raining. Before he put us out, he gave us specific instructions not to walk home from school if it was still raining. He said he would pick us up. Well, it was raining when school let out, but we elected not to heed his words. Our friends walked home, so we wanted to walk home as well. Of course, when my father went by the school to pick us up, we were not there. When he got home, he was mad at us because we failed to obey him. Although we stood in our soaked clothes, he instructed us to remove them and spanked us with his bare hands. My daddy had huge hands! It is one time I have never forgotten.

Much more than that one incident, I remember climbing up into my Daddy's lap countless times to kiss him. I also recall watching sports with him, being outside with him when he grilled, his taking us to McDonalds on Saturday mornings to eat breakfast, and going grocery shopping with him. To my friends he was a bear, but to me he was a gentle giant. I am sure there were times I probably deserved a whuppin (as we call them in the African-American community), but I did not get one. In other words, I deserved justice, but I received mercy instead. I believe because of the image I have of my natural father, I have a particular image of my heavenly Father. I know God to be gentle, and to exercise mercy when I know I do not deserve it. I deserve death, but somehow He gives me life. I was guilty, but mercy stepped in and exonerated me. I have been unable to explain it or take credit for it. All I know is, just like I climbed into my natural father's lap, I can always climb up into God's lap.

You too can climb into the Father's lap and it is not contingent on what you have or have not done. He always wants to be with you. He wants you to see Him as someone you can come to. In Hebrews 4:16, it says, "Let us therefore come boldly to the throne of grace that we may obtain mercy, and find grace to help in time of need." You can come to Him in supreme confidence, knowing you will not be rejected. You do not have to be afraid to ask Him for help because He wants to help you. Heaven has its ear to the floor waiting for you. If your image of God is distorted, it is never too late to get a accurate image of God, your Father. Pray with me:

Father, in Jesus' name, I thank You that I was created in Your very image and likeness. You have made me to reign. I am not anybody's door mat, but I represent the very best of who You are. Father, I thank You for the authority and dominion You have given me. Teach me how to be who You desire me to be. In Jesus' name, amen.

3
MIRROR MIRROR ON THE WALL
God Sees You in His Image and His Likeness

Did you know you were made in the very image of God? Yes, it is true. For some of us that is hard to believe, but no matter how hard it is to believe, it is a reality. God, in having a conversation with Himself said, "Let Us make man in Our image, according to Our likeness" (Genesis 1:26). In other words, God decided He wanted us to be just like Him so He created us to be replicas of Him, and gave us certain attributes that are relative to Him.

We all possess some level of creativity. Just as God created the heavens and the earth, each one of us has the ability to envision an idea and bring it to fruition. God designed you in such a way that your mind cannot contain all the dreams and ideas you have. I am a huge fan of Michael Jackson and one of the things I loved about him was his great sense of creativity. Jackson was so creative that it oozed out of him. In fact, once he told his mother, Katherine, he had a million songs in his head and those songs kept him up at night because he wanted so desperately to get them out. Wow, what creativity! You too have gifts and talents that are waiting to be unleashed. They have to be unleashed because when God got ready to make something, He had to do the same. When you understand that you have been made in the very image and likeness of God, you know you were born to create something. What idea is brewing inside you? What invention is waiting on you? How many of your dreams are waiting to be realized? The world is waiting on you!

How you see yourself is monumental. You are not a mistake. You are not less than anyone else. No one has the right to trample you. You are so powerful that what you say takes on a life of its own. When God spoke, things happened. When He said, "Let there be light," light appeared. We carry the same capacity inside of us. What we believe, we speak and what we speak becomes our reality. We must speak words of life to ourselves and about ourselves. Words are too powerful to be wasted on negativity. God, in His infinite power and wisdom, spoke what He wanted into absolute manifestation. We have the capacity to do the exact same thing. Why? Because God made us just like Him! Image is everything!

Once, a family member of mine made the statement that we come from a "poor family." I immediately resisted those words. My family is not poor and I refused to accept that poverty mentality for my life. I have too much creativity to accept poverty as the norm. I am one who believes we do not have to accept the negative words of others. I call them "word curses." I don't know about you, but I choose to accept what God says about me. Yes!

When God created you in His image and likeness, He also intended for you to rule. In other words, you were born to have dominion. This is why abuse, in any form, is unacceptable. You and I were not meant to be anyone's punching bag to pound, door mat to step on, or slave to bound. We were meant to walk in great authority. We are meant to succeed in life and not fail. When you know who you are and whose you are, you become who God intended for you to be. You become a winner. If a person is foolish enough to treat you less than special, then that person does not deserve you. Disconnect yourself from anyone who does not have the right image of you: an image of beauty, success, worth, value. Why do we let people treat us less than who we are? We do not see the best in ourselves. We are afraid to acknowledge that we are special and deserve to be treated as such. Sometimes we choose not to rule because we are either too afraid or do not think we have the capability, but because God made us, it is there. He has given us dominion (Genesis 1:30). It is not something that you picked up when you came out of your mother's womb. God gave it to you before you got here because He knew you would need it.

    The greatest image you can have of yourself is the one given to you by God. When I was a child it was always a constant argument in my mind, whether or not I was pretty enough. When I got older, it became an argument of whether I was attractive or not. Now, there are many times I look at myself in the mirror and remind myself how good I look. I am attractive and if I am not all that to someone else, then that is their problem. I believe I am God's gift to the world. What do you believe about yourself? Have you concluded that you have something to offer? Have you looked back on any past relationship and declared that it was the other person's loss? I have a message for all those who left me because they thought they could do better than me…bye. When you know that you have been made in the image of God, you learn the best of you is simply being you. You matter. You count. You have a uniqueness that no other human being has. No one can do you, but you. When you leave, the book will be closed because no one else can do what you do. Rock and Roll legend, Little Richard, had it right when talking about himself as "often imitated, but never duplicated!" You can never be duplicated, my friend. Never. Pray with me:

Father God, in the name of Jesus, You made me in Your image and Your likeness. I don't have to compare myself to anyone. I don't have to compete with anyone. I do not have to accept anyone's negative treatment of me. Thank You that You have made me special. I declare that I am who You say I am. I am good and very good. In Jesus' name, amen.

4
IDENTITY CRISIS 101
God Sees You as More Than a Conqueror

I have been here 40 years and so much of my life has been spent trying to figure out what was wrong with me. It all culminated for me one day when I found myself sitting in a psychiatrist's office looking up at the ceiling into the outer space of nowhere. I did not want to think I had made a mistake; after all I just needed to clear my head and deal with all my mental aches and pains. I went to the doctor hoping to discover why I was emotionally shattered. I wanted to know who or what had tarnished and damaged me many years ago. I needed to know why, at the age of four, my mental capacity had been hijacked by sexual fantasies of a stunningly beautiful cousin. I knew it had to be something deeply hidden in the crevices of my psyche. I was sick. My emotions had been severely punctured by isolation, rejection, and a love I thought had ruined me beyond repair.

I had it all figured out. I was going to walk into the doctor's office and tell him someone had violated me when I was a child and I wanted to know who. I wanted to be hypnotized so I could catch the culprit red-handed! What did I really expect to find? Did I really want to discover what I had longed to know? Are some secrets better left buried? Was I really ready for the very thing I thought I wanted to know? Hysterical and in a haste, I had to know why I had become the way I was. I was ready to point the finger and bind my life to every excuse I could find as to why I had become as a rollercoaster. Perhaps it was the beast that haunted my life as a child or maybe some sick person that violated my very innocence. As I sat with the psychiatrist session after session, what I longed to know never came, but what I feared stared me right in my face- ME. All of my questions as to why I had become fragile and a target for misery and pain were within me. It started with me.

I waited for the psychiatrist to take me on a journey into the depths of my subconscious and find what I had apparently buried, but I was never handed the shovel to unearth the great mystery of my life. I looked for some moment in my life where who or what would be revealed and punished by me, but my psychiatrist kept hitting me with hard questions.

He wanted to know how I could love someone who did not love me. How did I react when things did not go my way? After a few sessions, I wanted to know why we were still talking about me. This thing seemed to never turn away from me. My psychiatrist, seeing my frustration, said to me that before we can look at anyone else, I had to be willing to look at me, and if I am not able to do that, I may never know who, or what violated me.

Years later, I started having a recurring dream. In this dream, I was in my childhood home and no matter what the scenario, I always ran from the house, either through a window, or the front or back door. I ran away scared. I woke up in the same fear.

Once, in a dream, I walked toward my childhood home. I was about to go in, but a vicious dog stopped me. He told me I was not going into the house. Suddenly my pastor appeared, speaking with much authority, told the dog I was going into the house. As my pastor spoke, the dog became less hostile and retreated. The way was made for me to enter my house. Clearly, the way was made for me to deal with me, and to examine myself. I learned I had to go into my past to snatch my future. You might have to do the same. Even if it is of your own doing, whatever has crippled you must be met head on. Do not be afraid to confront what ails you! Actually, what *ails* you might one day *hail* you! You can rise above the very thing you thought you could never get over. If only we had the courage to face ourselves, and to look at who we *really* are. I ask you, who are you...really? Do you genuinely like who you have become? What secrets lie beneath the layers you have put on in an attempt to avoid facing reality? Is there something you really like and no one else knows about it but you? Is there something you hate that no one knows about? I implore you to take a leap of faith. Jump! Jump and discover the true beauty of who you are. I promise you, there is a whole world out there waiting for the real you to show up. Pray with me:

God, You know all things. You know my secrets. You know the dark and painful places of my life. You know every hurt and conflict I wrestle with. You are my

Father and I need You to help me face those things I have been too afraid to face- even me. Lord, I need courage and You are the only One that is able to give it to me. Father, help me face all of my giants and conquer all my fears. In the name of Jesus, amen.

5
ANOTHER MAN'S TREASURE
God Sees You as a Treasure

Inside of each of us is this need to feel wanted, to be significant to someone else, and to somehow be counted in the business of human affairs. What is also important is the constant need to right what we feel we have done wrong, and to fix ourselves if we find we are, in some capacity, broken. In fact, if we are not careful we can spend an entire lifetime trying to make up for mess ups and suck up for screw ups. We look backwards trying to undo what often cannot be undone rather than move forward and chart a new course. I have done what most have done. I felt if only I could get to the beginning of my life, I could undo it all. What if I told you that there is really no need to try and undo every mistake you have ever made? What if I said to you that your value has not depreciated despite what you have done or how you look at yourself? That the old saying, "one man's trash is another man's treasure" is really true?

I have dealt with hurt and rejection most of my life. Rejection and I were one. Every time I felt rejected, I felt unwanted, as a piece of discarded furniture. If you wanted to find me, you needed only to look on the side of the road. I was always out there just waiting to be picked up by some garbage man, whose job was to discard me into the landfill of life, or by the next person who saw I was good for something until I was no longer of use. It was a constant cycle. I felt worthless. I felt alone. I felt like trash. After years of always being one man's trash, and another's and another's, I discovered I will always be one man's treasure: God. I might be worthless to someone else, but I am worth something to God. I am His treasure and so are you! I do not care how many people trash you, God will always treasure you. He values you because He created you. Oh believe me when I tell you, it is wonderful and glorious to be adored by God!

I want you to get two words in your spirit when you think of all the people that did not think you were good enough: Their loss. When someone rejects you, consider it their loss. You do not have to walk around feeling sorry for yourself when you feel good about yourself. I have come to realize that if someone does not want me and what I have to offer, they are missing out on a "good thing!" You too are a good thing. God made you and He called everything He made, "very good" (Genesis 1:31).

None of us are trash because God created us. You deserve to be treated just as God created you. You are a treasure. You are to be treated as valuable, precious, rare, a jewel. I have concluded that I am like Haley's Comet. I only come around once in a lifetime. Catch me if you can. Pray with me:

God, I thank You that I am more precious to You than any jewel ever created. I thank You that I am what You treasure, above all things and I am grateful that You love me so much. Thank You Father for becoming so real in my life by showing me that I mean so much to You. You will never throw me away and love me too much to give me away. In Jesus' name, Amen.

6
YOU ARE A MASTERPIECE!
God Sees You as a Work of Art

For we are His workmanship, created in Christ Jesus for good works, which God prepared beforehand that we should walk in them. Ephesians 2:10

Close your eyes. Picture yourself in the finest museum in the world. You are not a patron, but you are the star attraction. People have lined up for hours in advance to see you and people have been awaiting your arrival for months, even years. As people enter the museum, there is an undeniable anticipation. Some have waited a lifetime to see you; you are their dream come true. Thousands stroll past you. You are a masterpiece!

The Apostle Paul referred to us in Ephesians 2:10, as "His (God's) workmanship." What a very interesting word and fascinating that God would define us, His very creation, as workmanship. The Greek word for workmanship is "poiema" (pronounced poy'-ay-mah) and is defined in the English language as "masterpiece" and "poem." God declares that we are His masterpiece and His poem. Hallelujah! We are the art and words of God Himself. We are His very expression. When He looks at you and me, He sees a masterpiece!

My twin sister has a degree in Art, so when God told me I was a masterpiece, I knew it was an art term. I started thinking about the painting, *Mona Lisa*.

The *Mona Lisa* is considered a masterpiece. If you look at the woman in the painting, she is not very pretty. I asked God how could someone that appears to be unattractive be worth so much. Today, the *Mona Lisa* is worth over $500 million dollars. Why is it worth so much? Why is it considered a masterpiece? *The Mona Lisa* is not a masterpiece because of Mona Lisa. *The Mona Lisa* is a masterpiece because of the one who painted it, Leonardo Da Vinci. Da Vinci was a famous painter, so whatever he painted is considered a masterpiece. If Da Vinci threw paint onto a canvas, it would still be a masterpiece. So, it is with you! God created you, so that alone makes you a masterpiece! It is not necessarily about us, the creature that makes us a masterpiece. It is the Creator. You might think you're ugly, too fat, or too skinny. You might even think you are nothing because of the color of your skin, or your sex, or your socio-economic status. Because God created you, you are a masterpiece and unlike the *Mona Lisa*, your value is too great to be measured! In the sight of God, the Federal Reserve cannot make enough money nor make it fast enough to get fair market value for any of us because when it comes to us, there is no such thing as fair market value. No one can afford you. There is no price that can be placed on you!

The *Mona Lisa* has been stolen and has experienced some level of damage on at least 4 different occasions. It was once doused with acid, had a rock thrown at it, sprayed by paint, and had a mug thrown at it. What does that say? There is always something or someone out to destroy a masterpiece. All the hurts, pains, and trauma you have endured are because forces of adversity have been out to destroy you. Even though the *Mona Lisa* has endured some damage over the centuries, some say it is the most valuable piece of art in the world. Damage to it has not diminished its value, and the same goes for God's creation. Nothing can depreciate us in His marketplace, so as we behold His glory, He beholds us.

Merriam Webster defines workmanship as, "the quality imparted to a thing *in the process of making*." In other words, not only are you a masterpiece because of the Creator (God), you were given a level of quality when God created you. I can just see Him, in my mind's eye, pouring the very best of Himself into us. Can you see it? While you were being formed by God, He gave you eminence. He gave you beauty. He gave you value. He gave you riches. You were made with the finest of things. I love it! Think of the most valuable, precious commodity in the earth and it stills trails in comparison to you. All the gold in the world cannot compare to you. You have been marked by God as His greatest creation and I declare your value just keeps going up and up and up! Pray this prayer with me:

Father, I thank You that it was You who created me. I thank You that You made me beautiful and special. I thank You that I am a masterpiece because You and You alone created me. Now let me see my own beauty and reveal to me my own self-value. I pray that every lie that was spoken over my life has been replaced with what You think about me. Amen.

7
POETRY IN MOTION
God Sees You as Beautiful Words

Not only does He refer to us as His masterpiece, God also called us a "poem." Personally, for me, this is significant because I love to write poetry. I love William Shakespeare. William Shakespeare is most famous for writing a particular form of poetry called a sonnet. A sonnet is a lyrical poem of 14 lines with each line containing 10 syllables. When I was in high school, we had to analyze a few of Shakespeare's sonnets. I scratched my head often because I had difficulty measuring the sonnet, finding the syllabic rhythm of it. You could only imagine the joy I felt when I was finally able to write my own sonnet. I asked God what does a 14 line poem (sonnet) have to do with me being His poem. What does the number 14 mean? The number 14 means, "To double or duplicate." Jesus said in John 14:12 (please note: it is written in the 14th chapter to his 12 disciples), "the works I do, you do, even greater works." God's intent for your life is for you to exceed even your own expectations. All limitations have been taken off! You live in the realm of limitless possibilities with the ability to supersede what others have done before you. You have been called into the extraordinary life! That's what "14" represents- the extraordinary! You are God's sonnet in the earth.

Another biblical example of double or duplication can be found in the life of Prophet Elisha.

Elisha was a student of Elijah, the great prophet of Israel. Elisha wanted a double portion of Elijah's spirit (II Kings 2:9). Elijah told Elisha he could have it if he saw him being taken away. Elisha was in fact present when Elijah was taken away, so he received a double portion of Elijah's spirit. Elijah performed seven miracles (1 Kings 17:1, 14, 22; 18:37-38, 41; 2 Kings 1:10, 2:8). In studying Elisha's miracles, I initially saw only 13 miracles. Puzzled, I thought if Elisha received a double portion of Elijah's spirit then Elisha should have performed 14 miracles. It perplexed me so much so that I counted Elisha's miracles over and over again because I certainly had missed one. I stumbled upon 2 Kings 13:20-21 and found Elisha's 14th miracle. I was so busy looking for the miracle in his life that I forgot what took place after Elisha's death. Elisha had been dead at least a year before his 14th miracle. Elisha was in the grave and the people brought a dead man to his grave and put him on top of Elisha. The man woke up and stood up on his feet. God's workmanship, His poem, had performed his 14th miracle and he did it from the grave! What does this say? You might be dead in your countenance; dealing with all sorts of mishaps and disappointments, but God can still use you, and it does not matter where you find yourself. Amen!

There is another form of poetry I want you to think of yourself as. It's called a haiku. A haiku might be the hardest poem to compose. I have written a couple of them over the years and it was very difficult. A haiku is a very interesting poem. It is of

Japanese origin and it also has a formula by which it must be written. If you do not write by it, it is not a haiku. A haiku is only 3 lines long, making it the shortest form of poetry, but it has a lot of substance in those 3 lines. It also has a rhythm of 7-5-7 syllables. One of the unique things about a haiku is there is no rhyme. Most people think that if a poem does not rhyme, it is not a poem. What the haiku says to you is you do not have to be like everybody else. You do not have to rhyme to reason. Is that not like our God? We spend our entire lives trying to be like someone else, but God always intended for us to chart our own course, and to be content with what He invested in us when He intricately designed us. Imagine our God sitting down to pen the bestselling book of all-time and when He finished, He had penned you. That's who we are! We are the best book of poetry ever written! We are God's compilation of poetry! Hallelujah! Pray with me:

Father, you have spoken about me into eternity. You said I am a poem. I can do that which I can imagine. I am greater than any poem created by any human being. You composed me, Father. Because You made me, I do not have to rhyme. You have made me to have my own unique substance. I thank You that I have not seen the best You have for me. Amen.

8
WHEN GOD MADE YOU!
God Sees You as His Original Design

You are a Designer's original. There is nobody like you in the entire universe- past, present, or future. One of my all-time favorite television shows is *The Jeffersons*. On one episode, George was named "Small Businessman of the Year" by a group of businessmen. His wife, Louise, eventually found out that George was not only being honored for his business savvy, but because he was small in statue as well. Two of the men from the organization stopped by to interview George, but he got called away on an emergency at one of his seven dry cleaning stores. One of the men said to Louise, "Thank God for the George Jeffersons of the world." Florence, the Jefferson's maid who always went toe to toe with George, stopped dead in her tracks when she heard this. Shocked she responded, "Oh, Lord! You mean there's more than one?" Though a funny observation by Florence, in reality, there can only be one George Jefferson and guess what, there can only be one of you!

People may try to emulate you, but you can never be duplicated. There is no carbon copy of you. Being a twin myself, I have met quite a few sets of twins in my day. Even if twins are identical, there is something distinctively different about them. There is not a set of identical twins that are exactly alike. The challenge of life for many of us is learning to be comfortable in our own skin. I have found that the reason we try to mimic others is because there is something we do not like about ourselves. We are always comparing ourselves to others, not realizing it is being who we are that makes us incomparable.

My favorite athlete of all time is Earvin "Magic" Johnson. What made him so unique is the fact that guys his size (6'9), do not play point guard. He was one of a kind. Just shy of a center in statue, he could rebound the ball, dribble it up the court without difficulty, and with gifted floor vision, could look at one guy and pass the basketball to another. His uniqueness made him do things guys his size could not do and no one has done since. He could have played power forward or center like most guys his size. He was in no way built to be a point guard, but that is what he excelled at. He was a point guard trapped inside a power forward or center's body. He was gifted with a unique skill set for his position. What if you and I exerted all of our energy into simply being who we were meant to be; mastered our skill sets? God is not looking for your mold in a material room to see if it fits some other human being. No! When you were created, He broke your mold because He had already created the best "you" possible when He made you! Nobody can do you. No one can be you. I really believe the reason we have celebrities is because they have mastered being who they are and normal people have not. There is only one Oprah. One

Michael Jackson. One Michael Jordan. There is only one you. Hallelujah! I get excited about that!

When I was growing up we would always hear the saying, "When God made you, He broke the mold." When it was used, it was usually used in a negative connotation. If we thought a person were ugly, it would imply no one is uglier. As God started to deal with me concerning my own self worth, both physically and emotionally, He said to me that when He made me He really did break the mold. Wow, I thought! There is no one in the world like me. Guess what else? There is no one else in the world like you, and not for the wrong reasons, but for all the right reasons! I believe that each one of us was born for a particular purpose and no one can carry out your purpose but you. Purpose cannot be transferred. It cannot be mistakenly given by God to you, then taken away and given to the right person.

I learned through this revelation that as soon as I start to accept my own uniqueness, the happier I will be. I spent too long trying to be like others that I wasted so many precious years of life- years I could have invested in discovering the beauty of me. Because I was born a twin, I always had someone to compare myself to. I failed to realize that if I would just see myself through the eyes of God, there is no one worthy enough to be compared to me. I am God's very own unique creation! If only we can get this reality through our heads, it will even affect how we allow others to treat us.

Psalms 139:14 speaks to our uniqueness in a most profound way. It says, "I will praise you Lord for I am fearfully and wonderfully made." It simply says that when God created us, He took His time. He was meticulous and precise. The phrase "fearfully and wonderfully made" means that God *skillfully* thought about you. He did not just snap his fingers and poof, you appeared. God, like a scientist, formulated a specific DNA for you. Like an architect, He saw you in His mind then drew you out as a blueprint. Like a potter, He shaped and formed you with His very hands. In all of this, God skillfully "wrought" you; meaning He was as a master welder. He physically welded you together piece by piece, and welded you together with your purpose. He specifically designed you and He specifically designed your purpose. He had a divine plan in mind when He made you. What a wonderful and powerful reality! Pray with me:

Lord God, You know my coming in and my going out. Thank You for making me wonderful, beautiful, and unique. Father, reveal to me my beauty even the more. Cause me to see what is special about me and help me to receive the love of others and to dismiss those who seek to abuse and mistreat me. You have created me with thought and fashioned me with precision. Thank you Father! In Jesus' name, amen.

9
BELOVED OF GOD
God Sees You as His Beloved

For years, there were two women I loved with all of my heart, at different periods of my life. I was sexually intimate with one for several years, and the other, I met as a teenager. We were close friends, but never intimate. Both relationships severely damaged me emotionally. I wanted both of them to love me, but I could not make either of them do so. So often when we want to be loved and we do not love ourselves, we cannot see when others do not love us. If we are not careful, we refuse to accept being unloved. Both relationships left me wondering what was wrong with me. What was it about me not to love?

Sadly, not only did I want the love of these two women, but I wanted their acceptance. With one, I longed so much for her acceptance that I felt inadequate without it. No matter how old I got, the teenager in me wanted to hear her say she was pleased with me. Otherwise, I felt like a failure. Once I had a dream I was running outside to get her attention, and not hearing me scream to her, she backed over me with her car. In reality, I had already finished college, authored a book, and was an ordained minister, but there I was running and screaming trying desperately to get her attention. She did not even hear me nor see me; she just ran over me. I stood in the dream and watched it unfold and it dawn on me how much of an emotional wreck I had become. No other human being deserves the right to have that much power over another human being. I can remember other days when I used to imagine hearing this one person say, "I am proud of you." I desperately wanted something I could not have.

The other woman came into my life later. From the first time I laid eyes on her, I think I was in love with her. Despite all the times we were intimate, she could not find it in herself to love me. When we were together, I would put all of my heart into pleasing her, but she just could not give her heart. I do not think she even tried. I brought the passion, and she brought her body parts with no strings attached.

I cried out to God because I started to internalize the pain of both of these relationships. I would get up in the middle of the night and sit on the side of my bed weeping because of the agony. The rejection was too great for me to bear. I would pray, "God help me to love me. Help me to know You love me." After all of that, I'd get pulled back in, only to repeat the same cycle in my other relationships.

When I set out for a relationship with God, things did not change overnight. I did not instantly and fully embrace God's love for me. I did not know how. It was something I had trouble accepting because I believed Him to be like all the others. I was so emotionally co-dependent that I was not sure if I knew what to do with His love anyway.

I asked God how He could love me. His answer was, "without conditions." Yes, God loves you too without conditions? You do not have to pretend or perform to get God's love. You do not have to be perfect, run with the right crowd, or have a certain amount of money. He loves you simply because He wants to.

I remember when I was in middle school at Highland Magnet School. My twin and I have always been popular, but we always had our own identity. As far back as I can remember, we never settled in with one particular group. We had friends in all circles. I think it was because of our upbringing. We were raised to think for ourselves, be creative, and to get along with all people. Our parents were Civil Rights Movement veterans, so even having white people in our home was normal. A group of girls (some of them were friends of ours) got together in middle school and started this club called The Sophisticated Ladies. My twin and I were not invited to join, for whatever reason. I guess we did not meet their expectations or something. My point is I may not have been qualified to be a Sophisticated Lady, but I am qualified to be God's lady and I do not have to be sophisticated. I say to you that God's love is an open invitation. It is not exclusive. He loves you so much and you do not have to be popular, down, or in to receive the amazing love of an amazing God!

There is absolutely nothing you can do to make God stop loving you or love you any less. You can be a rascal and He still loves you. It sounds so foolish, but it is unequivocally true. He knows you better than anyone else. I am convinced even when I laid my head in places I should not have, God still loved me. He feels the same about you! He loves you regardless- and there is nothing any one of us can do about it. We do not even have to accept it. It is what it is.

I was praying once and God spoke to me through His Word. He called me, "beloved of God." I melted like ice cream on a hot summer's day. His words were as real to me as a conservation I could have with anyone. His words weaken me to a place of great healing. I have sat on the side of my bed many times following that encounter and asked Him to teach me how to embrace His love. I did not know how to embrace the love of God because I had been hurt so badly too many times. Surely, I thought, He was like everyone else! We often cannot embrace the things of God because we have been so disappointed by others. If you have been hurt like me, you probably have found it difficult to accept God's love for you as well. I can tell you that it is His love that heals us from all the hurts of others. He wants to go into every dark place of our lives and give us light.

I love Tyler Perry. His movies are great teaching tools. There is a scene in his movie adaption of Ntozake Shange's, *For Colored Girls Who Have Considered Suicide When the Rainbow Is Enuf* that gives an example of the very love of God. Crystal Wallace, played by actress Kimberly Elise, is in deep grief over the death of her two children. The children's father was a hopeless alcoholic and in a rage, he threw the children from the window of a high rise apartment complex. Crystal is so grief stricken that she just stays in her apartment in the dark. One day, her neighbor Gilda, played by Phylicia Rashad, came over to check on her. She walked into a dark filled room. Gilda went over to the window, pulled back the curtains, and sunlight suddenly came beaming through. God's love is like that sunlight. His love permeates. God's love meets us no matter where we find ourselves. Whether we are grieving the loss of a loved one, feeling deserted, or mad at our circumstances, He knows exactly where we are. Even when we fail, He loves us through our failures. His love is a dichotomy. He loves the worst of each of us and He loves the best of us. This is why He calls you, "beloved." I believe He used *beloved* because no human being can ever love another human being to that dimension. Beloved means, "greatly loved." God does not just love you and me, but He *greatly* loves us. His love for us is so great; it cannot be measured. It overflows every boundary. No dam can control it. It can meet you on the mountaintop and rescue you in a valley. Hallelujah, His love cannot and will not be contained!

Wow! God says He greatly loves us! It is a promise and we have to remind ourselves that He greatly loves us. Remind yourself daily. It is that kind of love that keeps us from losing our minds. You are truly the apple of His eye (Psalm 17:8). Pray with me:

Father, thank You that You love me so much! Father teach me to accept Your love and know in my heart that You love me unconditionally. Thank You Father that there is nothing I can or cannot do to deserve Your love nor can anything separate me from Your love. I thank You that You have called me Your Beloved. In the name of Jesus, amen.

10
THE GIFT OF YOU
God Sees You as a Gift He Gave to the World

Have you ever said about someone or heard someone say about you, "Who does he (she) think he (she) is? God's gift to the world?" Usually that statement is being said by someone who is feeling insecure about herself but, guess what? You are God's gift to the world! You have been uniquely designed by God, so being the best you is your greatest calling. Embracing who you are is empowering you. Because God created you, there is something great and impactful about you. I want to take it a step further: All of the things you have had to endure are in direct correlation to the greatness inside you. I believe to the degree you have suffered or struggled is a reflection of your very awesomeness. Hallelujah! All your mess has conspired to give you a message that no one else can deliver, but you! You represent the best of God and that is something life does not want to be revealed.

The worst of life can be thrown at you, hit you, and you can still come out on top. I was bullied as a child. The bully actually was a friend of mine. Some days we walked home from school and she would not bother me. Other days I was the center of her abuse. She would push, punch, hit, and constantly pick on me. She was about twice my size and bigger than everybody else. I was skinny with a stuttering problem so I guess I was a pretty good target. Later in life, I realized she was a tool to keep me from being who I was destined to be. Perhaps it was not my insecurity alone she was after, but it was her own insecurity she was trying to mask. In some sordid way, when she punched me, she was really punching at what she hated about herself. I came to realize that whatever the reasons, it was something unique about me that life wanted to conceal from me. Believe me or not, but I am convinced that many of us are just like Moses. Moses' parents saw this very thing about him and it propelled them to act.

Hebrews 11:23 says, "By faith Moses, when he was born, was hidden three months by his parents, because they saw he was a *beautiful* child; and they were not afraid of the king's command." The word, "beautiful" is not in reference to his physical appearance, but his parents saw he was different, unique, special, and not ordinary. Pharaoh sent out a decree that all the male babies, three years old and younger, had to be killed, but Moses' parents perceived his uniqueness so they protected him from being killed.

Because God created you in His own image, you possess the same uniqueness as Moses. You have been released into the earth to impact it in such a way that only you can. We used to say, "God don't make no junk," so when He made you, He made a jewel. He made something so precious that even the heavens have to stand up and applaud you, and hell has to acknowledge you. All the hell you have been through is to shield what is beautiful and wonderful about you. The bruises of life are a mirage and an illusion. Even the darkest moments of your life are meant to be a light for someone else. God would not have it any other way. He knows us and He knows we can overcome any obstacle. No other creation has the mind capacity to do such a thing! You do! You can! It is why the greatest gift of your uniqueness can be summed up in one word: YOU. Nobody can do "you" but "you." It is something you cannot be afraid to embrace. Accept it now. Make peace with who God made you and how being you can best serve the world. You are the best offer. All competitors have been defeated when you conquer your fear of being you. Too often we upset the natural order of things because we settle for mediocrity. Mediocrity is when we decide to follow everybody else rather than dance to the beat God distinctively put inside each of us. Henry David Thoreau said, "If a man does not keep pace with his companions, perhaps it is because he hears a different drummer. Let him step to the music which he hears, however measured or far away." God's intent is for you to maximize what He invested in you. He wants you to succeed.

Just as God equipped Adam with everything he needed to succeed, He equipped you. God gave Adam a place to dwell, empowered him to make critical decisions, and even gave him a mate to help him complete his assignment. He did the very same thing for you and me. All of us have been given as a gift. Adam was a gift to the Garden of Eden. Genesis

2:15 says, "Then the Lord God took the man and put him in the garden of Eden to tend and keep it." God made the Garden first, but needed Adam to manage and oversee it. God needs you to manage His purposes. He sent you into the earth as a gift to the earth and mankind.

There is not a single person born into the world by accident. You are an absolute certainty. You may be a person that calls into question the "how" of your existence, but make no mistake about it, you are intentional. It does not matter how you got here, you are here. You are here to make a difference. You are here to fulfill your God-given purpose. Find it in Him. Search it out in Him. You owe it to yourself to release your beauty, gifts, and talents into the lives of others. It took me years to intimately know I am a gift. For as long as I could remember, I always felt awkward and out of place. Even in a room filled with people, I felt odd. Just as I struggled with those feelings, I desperately attempted to fit it. I never did and the more I tried the more miserable I became. One day I stopped fighting. You too can stop fighting! Stop fighting all the things you think are wrong with you. The greatest gift you can give anyone is the gift of simply being who you are. You cannot be someone else. God knows I have tried! I thought if I could have what someone else has or if I could be someone else, all of my worries and insecurities would dissipate. When I discovered I possessed certain strengths and gifting that the world needed, I started to love and appreciate myself even the more.

One thing I have always loved is seeing people laugh or have a good time. Even when I hated myself, I always managed to say something funny to get those around me to laugh. When I was a child, my maternal grandmother, Mary, used to get on me all the time because every time she looked around, I was giggling. As I got older, I still giggled a lot and always had a wise crack, joke, or sarcasm for everybody. In an attempt to change, I tried to become more serious. I did not wear being serious well and the more I tried to be serious, I felt miserable and out of place. I had to be me. I had to come to grips with the reality that being funny is a part of who I am. It is at the very core of my person. All of us have to embrace who we are and find solace in the fact that it is really alright to be you. You are a gift and when you allow yourself to be unwrapped from all pressure, pretensions, and perceptions of others; you open yourself to unlimited possibilities and immense peace.

When you are free, you free others. Pray with me:

Father God, in the name of Jesus, cause me to know I am special. Thank You for revealing Your love to me in a real way. I am grateful that You made me and I did not make myself. God, heal me from all forms of rejection, disappointment, and my need for unhealthy love. Cause me not to give myself to people who do not deserve to have me in their lives. Teach me how to love and appreciate myself. In Jesus' name, amen.

11
THE HEIR APPARENT
God Sees You as Royalty

"And Esau said, look, I am about to die so what is this birthright to me. Then Jacob said swear unto me as the day and Esau swore unto him and sold him his birthright to Jacob." Genesis 25:29

Whenever we feel we do not belong or we are less than someone else, we give in. We feel what we want is taking absolutely too long or life has been full of delays and regrets. We get weary. That is what happened to Esau. He got weary, and when he got weary, he sold his birthright. Esau was the first born of Isaac's twins. Jacob was the other twin. In Jewish culture, the firstborn child is the first heir of the father. There are certain things bestowed upon the firstborn, particularly the son. Esau was a hunter who had gone out to the field to catch game. Jacob knew that it was a great thing to be the firstborn son because he understood the privileges that went along with it. Knowing his brother would be weary from the hunt, Jacob knew Esau would also be very hungry. Jacob had a bowl of stew waiting on Esau. Esau begged Jacob for the stew and because he was so famished and did not know the value of the birthright, Esau sold it to Jacob for the stew. When we do not know who we are, we sell ourselves and what is rightfully ours. We settle for anything. I can always tell when a person's self-esteem is in the tank. How? By the people they connect to. A king will hook up with a prostitute if he has low self-esteem. You become what you believe about yourself. Esau lowered the value of his birthright to a bowl of stew! He sold his destiny for something that was temporal. Weariness does not last always, and what normally happens is we get had by someone who sees our value. The birthright was valuable to Jacob. He knew it could unlock his destiny and he knew the birthright did not mean anything to Esau. Jacob knew exactly what to ask for. When you do not love yourself, you become the prey of another man's hunt when you were intended to be the heir apparent.

Do not sell you birthright. When you don't know who you are, you sell yourself short. After Esau sold his birthright, he immediately became bitter. At first he wanted to die because he was so hungry, but then he really wanted to die when he realized what he had done. He discovered who he was and his own significance too late. In consequence, he discovered who he was after Jacob. It is a sad thing to wallow in the abyss of self-pity and self-doubt, while other people regard your kingly position. Others know you are a king, but the king does not know he is a king.

The great tragedy, in my opinion, is not only did Esau fail to recognize his kingly position (heir), but he also failed to realize that he was a *son*. Esau acted more like a slave than a son. When God looks at you, He sees a son (or daughter). You are not a slave. You do not have to sit around and ask for permission to be- you already are. The book of Galatians makes it clear that we are sons of God. The book of Romans states that we are "heirs of God and joint heirs with Christ Jesus." In other words, we have an inheritance. You have an inheritance and since Christ has already died, the will and testament has already been read. All things are yours! Hallelujah! As Jonathan put a kingly robe on David (1 Samuel 18:4), so God has done to all of us. You are the very seed of God. He has robed you with all rights and privileges. Pray with me:

Father, make me know who I am in You and value all that You have given me. Help me not to take what You have blessed me with lightly. Cause me to cherish and value all that You have placed into my hands. Father, thank You for believing in me and for giving me an inheritance. Thank You Father, I am not a slave, but I am a son. If I do not know how to be a son, teach me so that I may walk in it. In the name of Jesus, amen.

12
IN THE HANDS OF THE POTTER
God Sees You as Clay in His Hands

And the vessel that he made of clay was marred in the hand of the potter: so he made it again another vessel, as seemed good to the potter to make. Jeremiah 18:4 (NKJV)

When Femi and I were growing up, my parents always made sure we were in some type of arts program. I assumed it was because we displayed so much creativity early on and they felt it needed to be fostered so they invested. One of the classes, and I will never forget it, was a pottery class. We loved it so much our parents bought us our very own pottery wheel. When you first start with clay, you get this square block of clay. The first thing you do is get a feel for the clay by working, mashing, and pulling it. It starts out soft and in order to keep it soft, water must be applied to it. Sometimes, I already had in mind what I wanted to make with the clay so I tried to work the clay down to some type of starting point. I did not always know what I was doing. Unlike that initial block of clay, you have never been a block of clay in the mind of God nor have you ever been an empty canvas. In my house, my sister has some canvases with nothing on them, unknown to the artist, but not so with you and me. In Jeremiah 1:5, God said to Jeremiah that, "before I *formed* you in the womb I knew you." Like Jeremiah, you already were before your parents even conceived you. You have *never* been unmade or unformed. God has always had us in His mind. What does this mean? The word "nothing" in the context of who we are should not be a part of our vocabulary. Zero may be a number, but it should not be applied to our personal worth and self-value. Stop telling yourself, "I'm nothing!" You have never been a nothing! You have always been important in God's mind. It does not really matter how we were born and under what circumstances because we already were before. Our parents were conduits that God used to get us into the earth to do great things.

Many of us, in some form or another, have been marred by life. It is one of the things that connect us as human beings. Each one of us has a story to tell. I call them precious jewels, also known as "life experiences." I once heard Dr. Rita Twiggs make a profound statement. She proclaimed, "No one lays down a blunder and wakes up a wonder." This is so true. Often times what we fail to do is take what happened to us and let it make us into something so beautiful. We are God's creation and He chose to send us to earth, into time. Hold up! Into time? Yes, God sent us into time, or better yet, I should say "life." We were with Him in eternity. When we are born, we are placed into time. Time produces a lot of things: hurt, success, pain, joy, failure, fear, faith. You name it, our lives have produced it, but the beauty of it all is that it is meant to produce a story someone else can read. All the things that have marred us are supposed to motivate someone else. When someone looks at our lives no matter how bad we think it has been, it is still meant to give life to someone else. That is the beauty of being in the hands of the Potter Himself! Pray with me:

Father God, I thank You that You are the Potter in my life. You have made me with Your very hands. Father, thank You that You have made all things to work together for my good, according to Romans 8:28. I thank You for seeing value in me and seeing value in all the things I have gone through. You have made me a vessel to be used to bless others. Lord I thank You for all things that have happened in my life. In Jesus' name, Amen.

13
STICKS & STONES
God Sees You as a Word Out of His Mouth

If we have heard it once, we have heard it a thousand times more: "Sticks and stone may break my bones, but words will never hurt me." We spewed these words when we were children, but as soon as we hit adulthood we come to realize how every negative word ever spoken to us or about us is crippling. I have had a lot of physical scars in my life especially while growing up. I fell off of my bicycle, played too rough at times, and got involved in neighborhood scuffles. Those wounds eventually healed, but the wounds of name calling, insults, jokes, and ridicule have taken almost a lifetime to heal, and in some cases are still healing. It is the things we say and the things that are said to us that produce feelings of inadequacy and self-loathing. Negative words make us far more impotent than any drug we could ever take. Negative words produce an atmosphere over our lives just as positive words do. Negative words produce oppression and make us feel as if we will never be good at anything. This is why relationships become so important, especially as we get older. I always say a relationship has so much power, because they can do one of two things: make you feel like you are standing on top of the world or make you feel like the world is on top of you. Excuse negative people from your life because it will dictate where you go in life. You can only soar if you are around other eagles!

We are all products of the words spoken over our lives. I believe to some degree, we are words manifested in the form of flesh. This is why Jesus proclaimed, "My words they are spirit and they are life" (John 6:63)! He was the manifested "Word" of God in the earth. Everything God had spoken, He became the manifestation. He had heard all the right things, received affirmation and confirmation from the Father, and what He heard from the Father He manifested in the earth. The opposite effect can be found in the life of Jabez.

It was said of Jabez that he was more honorable than all his brothers, but his mother endured so much pain during his birth that she named him Jabez. 1 Chronicles 4:9 records, "Now Jabez was more honorable than his brothers, and his mother called his name Jabez, saying, 'Because I bore him in pain.'" I imagine Jabez lived with the curse of his "pain" for years. I can only envision the pain he felt every time he heard his name called. If your name has a meaning, every time someone calls your name, they are releasing the meaning of it into the atmosphere. Be careful what you name your children! I always say my parents hit the jackpot when they named me. Although, people have made fun of it over the years and acted ignorant about it, I would not change it for the world. Why? I know what it means. Bummi is Nigerian and it means, "A gift has been given." Every time I hear it called, I do not just hear my name, but I hear its meaning as well. I love it! Now, do not get me wrong, I have also had to deal with the negative things that happen to a gift as well, such as being rejected, unappreciated, and not valued. I have also felt the good. What is most important in all of our life experiences is our response. What do we do with all the negative words we have heard? How do we navigate through all the mess and find some solace? Jabez had the proper response. He went to his first parent, God Himself:

And Jabez called on the God of Israel saying, "Oh that You would bless me indeed, and enlarge my territory, that Your hand would be with me, and that You would keep me from evil, that I may not cause pain!" So God granted him what he requested. 1 Chronicles 4:10

Jabez did what we all must do. He went to the One that had created him and knew all about him. Jabez's mother bore him in pain, but he went to the One that bore him in joy before his mother and father ever got together. God's word about you supersedes any word ever spoken over your life, so it does not matter what the bully on the block called you or what the husband (wife) who left you said about you. I ask you, what does God say about you? It is a question only you can answer. Pray with me:

Father, I thank You that I am a word spoken out of your very mouth before the foundation of the world. Every negative word that has been spoken over my life by others, I reject right now. I reject word curses that have been unleashed over me (and my seed) in the name of Jesus. I plead the blood over what You have said about me and I ask that You continue to tell me what I am and who I am. Reveal your thoughts about me O God. Thank You Father that you know me and I am special to You. In Jesus' name, amen.

14
THE MIND OF GOD
God Sees You as One He Thinks About All the Time

R& B singer, Babyface, had something when he penned the words, "I only think of you on two occasions. That's day and night." It was truly a love song for the ages. I like the song because it gives me a clue to the fact that God thinks of us day and night. Yes! We are forever on the very mind of the Almighty God! Hallelujah! Psalm 8:4-5 says, "What is man that You are mindful of him, and the son of man that You visit him? For You have made him a little lower than the angels, and You have crowned him with glory and honor."

There is not a moment that God does not have each of us on His mind. His eye is a watchful one and he thinks about us all the time. Even when I was a child I felt God was watching me. I could not explain it, but I always felt I was the center of the universe. It sounded crazy then, and although I could not articulate it, I felt God's eyes on me. I compared it to someone watching me while I was on TV. It just felt like I was never alone even if I was alone. Of course, my feeling this way always left me with a lot of questions about God. I knew I just did not spring up into existence. I was sent into the world.

God's eyes are on you! He knows your thoughts, dreams, and fears. He knows what you like and what you despise. There is nothing that goes on in your life that does not have God's attention. He intimately thinks about you. I believe He never sleeps because He is too busy thinking about you. It is like being in love. Every time I was in love, I could not sleep. I would try, but I would always find myself thinking about the person I was in love with, even if the person did not know I felt that way. At times, I would lie awake fantasizing about the person, wondering what they were doing. I wanted to express my love for them. God is the same way! He wants us to know He loves us and wants to express that love in a very real way. I also can remember wishing that special person would call me, no matter when, day or night. God desires the same. He wants us to talk to Him. He wants to talk to us. He longs for us. He weeps for us. He desperately wants us.

I want you to think about the most critical times in your life. Perhaps, it was a time of feeling unloved, unwanted, lost, or grieved. Or perhaps you lost everything you own in a divorce or a horrific accident. God is ever present and He is most concerned about you. He is in love with you.

You stay on God's mind. Before you laugh at the notion, God's very thoughts about you are so good. You mean the absolute world to Him. There is not a creature alive that has God's attention more than you and me. You can rest assure that what concerns you, concerns God and He is working things out for your good. You can believe that! Let's pray:

Father, You have spoken. I thank You that I am always on Your mind. I am grateful that You have plans to give me a hope and a future, according to Jeremiah 29:11. God, teach me how to walk with You and intimately know that Your thoughts toward me are good. In the name of Jesus, amen.

15
You're No Ugly Duckling!
God Sees You as Beautiful

When I was a kid I watched a film called *The Ugly Duckling*. I remember sitting there in my classroom at seven or eight years old, watching this story that apparently had some kind of meaning or value to life. Now in my adult life, things look even clearer. I have discovered its relevance.

There was this family of ducks, including the mother and her six ducklings. They traveled the pond together, riding along in a row. As the film went on, the mother and her ducks were swimming along in the pond: five beautiful, white ducks, all together. As they passed, the camera stayed its position so much so that even a seven year old knew something else was coming. As the camera stood still, into the picture came another duckling, away from the pack and looking nothing like the others. The narrator of the film referred to him as *the ugly duckling*. In my young mind, I readily agreed, as well as the rest of my classmates.

The duckling was so "ugly" that his siblings did not want him around and the mother duck did little to encourage them to invite him in or make him feel a part of the family. So the ugly duckling depressingly went about, feeling left out, unwanted, and unloved. Every time you saw them traveling the waters, you saw him trailing behind. As time went on, something amazing happened! Eventually the duckling became a beautiful swan, but even in its beauty it remained unlike the others. They gathered around him and made him a part of the family. They accepted him and he became the most beautiful swan to behold of them all, but keep in mind, he remained unlike the others. As I have matured, I see this story in a different light.

What if the duckling was seen, from the beginning, as different? Not ugly. Yes, different! The duckling did not look like the other ducklings. The other ducklings were yellow, but he was all white, so he was seen as ugly and unattractive. What if we were all taught that story from the perspective of being different rather than ugly? I bet we would be a nation of people who didn't mind standing out from the crowd, unafraid of being who we are and doing what we were called to do. In fact, Jesus would have been labeled an ugly duckling because He too was different.

Have you ever been called the ugly duckling of your family, of your classmates, or your co-workers? Or perhaps you are a minister and you are so unlike the brethren. Have you been separated from them because you do not look or sound anything like them? Do you feel awkward in the midst of everyone you are around? You just do not fit in and because you know you do not fit, you think there is something wrong with you? Somehow a mistake was made? Yes, I know the feeling.

I have thought all these things from the very early stages of my life. I never fit in, so much so that I tried desperately to. From the first grade to college and even into adulthood, I thought I was a realistic version of *The Ugly Duckling* until I discovered that I am not ugly. I am different. I am not made to fit in.

Stop trying to be like everybody else! You and I were never meant to be like anybody else. God is so sovereign that He would not let us be like that anyway. He wants us to be unique and peculiar! When we realize this, we will become as the duckling in the story. We too will be transformed into beautiful swans. Pray this prayer:

God, You have made me. You made me beautiful (handsome) and wonderful. I thank You for creating me and making no one else like me. Help me to embrace it. Cause me to know I was created to be different and not like everybody else. Thank You Lord for making me who I am. In the name of Jesus, I pray, amen.

16
AND PETER
God Sees Your Failures as Steps to Success

Nobody likes to fail and I do not think any of us set out to do it. It happens and we as human beings have a tough time coming to grips with the fact that we are not perfect. I think what we wrestle with more than anything is how we think others will perceive us when we fail. All of us have this need to be accepted and want to be viewed in a positive light. We do not realize that failure can be a tool in our process, and although it may disqualify us in the arena of public opinion, it may qualify us in God's arena.

I know you are probably shaking your head at my previous point because you think I have made a blasphemous statement, but I believe it is true. There are two truths I have found in the Word of God: it is a book about God's plan for redemption and it is a book filled with imperfect people. Salvation itself is about the need for a perfect God. I believe if you cannot see your own imperfection as a human being, then you need to evaluate your salvation because Christ died for your sins i.e. your imperfections.

For me, perhaps the greatest example of failure in the Word of God can be found in the life of Peter. Peter had some great experiences with Christ. It was Peter who walked on the water to meet Jesus. Peter also was the one disciple who proclaimed that

Jesus was the Christ, the Son of the living God. Peter, in my opinion, was the most protective of Jesus because he cut off a man's ear in the Garden of Gethsemane when Jesus was taken into custody. Peter was a bad boy and as loyal as they come! But in his moment of great testing, Peter failed. How many times have we failed? I have countless times. As Jesus Christ was getting ready to be crucified, he talked with the disciples about what was to come. He warned them that all of them would forsake him and leave him. Peter, being so loyal, declared he would never leave Jesus. Jesus, having already seen what was to come, told Peter he was going to deny him as surely as the rooster crowed three times (Luke 22:33-34). He also told Peter that Satan had asked for him so that Satan may sift him as wheat (Luke 22:31). When the moment came, he did exactly what Jesus told him he would do. Peter was so distraught that the Word of God says he, "wept bitterly." Even though Peter had failed, I believed that failure made him the great apostle he would become more than anything else he ever did. When it came time for him to deny Christ again on the day of Pentecost, he stood boldly and proclaimed God's Word and bore witness to Jesus, the Resurrected Savior, and the outpouring of the Holy Spirit (Acts 2:14:41). Just because Peter failed, it did not disqualify him from the work he was destined to do. In actuality, as Jesus had also seen Peter deny Him, He also saw his conversion and his redemption. What we can learn from Peter's failure is that God already knows when and how we are going to fail. Your failure is not a surprise to God. You may or may not know you are going to fail at something, but God knows, and He knew it before the world was formed.

The one thing I have always loved about Peter's situation is God restored him in such a powerful way. I call it the, "And Peter" moment. An angel appeared after Jesus' resurrection, at His tomb. The angel instructed the women to gather the disciples together in Galilee so Jesus could meet with them before He ascended to heaven. In doing so, he specifically said to them, "Go tell His disciples *and Peter*" (Mark 16:7). He wanted Peter to know he mattered; he was still included in the plan of God. Jesus knew Peter was out there in the wind, having committed a colossal failure. He knew Peter had withdrawn and isolated himself, so He made sure that whatever he had to tell the others, He had to tell Peter also. Powerful! I say to you that no matter your failure, God has not cast you to the side. God has not excommunicated you from His plans. He needs you and wants you to do what He called you to do. As a matter of fact, when Jesus talked directly to Peter (John 21:15-17), He asked, "Peter, do you love Me?" Peter answered yes. Jesus did not reply, "Good. Don't do it again!" He replied, "Feed my sheep." He empowered Peter. He did not lambast him. No matter what you have done, God is not lambasting you. He forgives you. He loves you, plain and simple. I say to you as Jesus said to Peter just before the denial: when you are converted, strengthen others (Luke 22:32).

Failure should convert you. In other words, it should change your life for the better. Your personal failure is supposed to strengthen others. People should learn from our mistakes. It is the one thing that identifies us with the human experience. I cannot tell you the number of times I have had someone come up to me and say I blessed them because I was not afraid to be vulnerable about my own frailties. Again, it is our mess that gives us a message. It is what gives life and hope to others. When God looks at you, He sees someone He can use. No matter the failure, you are usable to God. God certainly does not think like we think. He knows how to take the broken pieces of our lives and make us *again.* He took Abraham's mistake with Ishmael and still fulfilled the promise He had made him in Isaac. He took Noah, an alcoholic, and used him to preserve the earth while it rained 40 days and 40 nights. Though David sinned against God with Bathsheba, He still used him and out of David came the wisest king ever, Solomon. The Apostle Paul had something he referred to as a "thorn." It is one of Christianity's unknown mysteries as to what Paul's thorn was, but whatever it was, God told him, "My grace is sufficient for you, for My strength is made perfect in weakness" (2 Corinthians 12:9). What is it in your life that needs the very grace of God applied to it? No matter what you have done, you cannot do enough for God to change His mind about you. You mean more to Him than you will ever know.

Failure is a tool. Every tool has a distinct function. What you and I have to do is find out how we can best let our failures work for us and know that God's job is to cover us despite our mistakes. We cannot fix it ourselves. Adam and Eve tried to fix it themselves. When they disobeyed God, they hid themselves from the very presence of God because they were ashamed and feared the wrath of God. God, in his compassion, sewed fig leaves together and covered them. Their response was not sufficient. If their response was sufficient, God would not have made provision for them. If you have failed at something, the blood of Jesus has made it possible for you get back up, dust yourself off, and move forward. Just as God saw the best in Peter, He sees the best in you. He has written the script on you and surely, it has a happy ending. Pray with me:

Father, I thank You that You have allowed failure in my life. Now cause me to grow from it and teach others what I have learned. Father, help me to release all hurts, disappointments, failures, mistakes, and pains. All of it is working for my good. Heal me Lord as only You can. In Jesus' name, amen.

17
WALK ON WATER!
God Sees You as a Water Walker

In the eyes of God, all of us are like Peter. We too can walk on water! Yes! I do not think in the mind of God, there is not one thing we cannot do. He believes in us more than we believe in ourselves. Jesus proved His faith in Peter more than once and one night in particular, the courage of Peter was born.

Matthew 14:22-33 records that one night Peter and the rest of the disciples were hanging out on the seas. I can imagine them sitting around on the boat talking and sharing when they saw what looked like a ghost out on the water. It was not a ghost. It was Jesus. Peter asked Jesus if it was Him to let him come out on the water with Him. Jesus invited Peter. Peter stepped out of the boat and walked on the water toward Jesus. Peter did not walk *in* the water, he walked *on* the water. How in the world was Peter able to walk on water? I believe he walked on the water because he was willing to do what nobody else was willing to do. He simply asked Jesus to let him come and then he went. There is no record where any other disciple asked Jesus for permission to come out to meet him on the water. When you are willing to do what you think you cannot do, God is going to have a front row seat because He knows you can do it. Anybody can walk in the water. Walking in the water is safe, especially if you can swim. When you walk in the water, you have become like everybody else. You have consented to mediocrity, but when you walk on the water, you catapult yourself into another realm! Peter did just that and so can you.

God wants us to do the amazing! Whatever you think you cannot do in your life, do it! You owe it to yourself and believe me, you will be much happier. Now when you decide to take that step of great faith, be prepared to be met with opposition. While Peter was walking on the water, the Word of God says, "But when he saw that the wind was boisterous, he was afraid; and beginning to sink he cried out, saying, 'Lord, save me'" (Matthew 14:30)! When we give attention to negativity, doubt, fear, the opinions of others, wrong mindsets (boisterous winds), we take our focus off of God and His investment in us. We become fearful and retreat right back into a state of normalcy. When Peter realized the winds were getting stronger, he panicked and began to sink. Oh, how many times I started to sink when trouble arose in my life. I encourage you to ignore the naysayers. God has equipped you to do something great. Do it!

Often what sets us apart from regular folks is the courage to try, even if we fail. Peter had great courage to step out of the boat. The other eleven decided they would rather kick back and relax. Chill. Play it safe. I can only imagine what they thought about Peter when Jesus invited him. One of them probably tried to pull him back and told him he was crazy. Another probably reminded him that what he was attempting to do had never been done before, so do not do it. A third one perhaps warned him about drowning and reminded him he could not swim. Another disciple possibly discouraged him because if he succeeded, he would be the talk of the town. Maybe another pleaded with Peter not to get out of the boat because he did not want Peter to change. Or another was too afraid himself to take a chance so Peter had no right to.

All of us have had to contend with dissenting voices, whether without or within. Do not spend your time trying to convince those against you to get on your side. Do not even bother trying to justify why you are doing what you are doing because few of us are willing to do something we have never done in the first place. Surround yourself with people, who are not afraid to chart new courses and who are willing to do what has never been done. Study those who have pioneered new landscape. God has invested so much in you that you owe it to yourself to at least try. Though he sank, Peter tried. He attempted to do what seemed impossible. I challenge you to try than not try at all.

When Peter started to sink, Jesus caught him and they got into the boat. When they got back into the boat, *the winds ceased* (Matthew 14:32). When you conform to someone else's perception of you, there is little resistance. When you decide to be like everybody else rather than be who God created you to be, the warfare ceases. It is comfortable in the boat. Nothing is happening in the boat. There is no immediate threat or impending danger in the boat. If you have settled for staying in the boat with everybody else, God is calling you to get out of the boat. He wants you to walk on water. He knows you can do it because He has put Himself in you!

Let the winds of opposition blow. If you are in the right position, the wind just might be at your back. And if it is at your back, let it push you right into your God-given destiny. Hallelujah! Let's pray:

Father, give me the courage of Peter to try something I have never done. Help me to trust You and turn a deaf ear to all that oppose me. I have Your DNA so I can do anything! Thank You Father, for believing in me. In Jesus' name, amen.

18
Lights! Camera! Action!
God Sees Your Story as a Made for Life Movie

We often equate what is going on in our lives with whether God loves us or not. If things are going bad, we think God is mad with us. If things are going good, we must be on good terms. It is hard for us to believe that if we are having a tough time, the tough time will make us better. I know a man named Joseph. He was a dreamer and his dreams signaled to him that he was going to be great. In one of his dreams, even his family bowed down to him. One day he made a mistake and told his brothers and father about the dreams. He made his brothers mad, but his father, Jacob, knew there was some validity to the dreams. Jacob also loved Joseph more than he loved his brothers. He loved Joseph so much that he gave him a unique coat. There was not one like it anywhere. Joseph's brothers hated him even more because Jacob loved Joseph. The brothers decided to get rid of Joseph, so they kidnapped him and planned to kill him, but one of the brothers, Reuben, pleaded with the other brothers not to kill Joseph. They opted instead to put him in a pit. They then sold him into slavery. Nowhere in Joseph's dreams was it revealed to him that he would first end up in a pit, be sold as a slave, and end up in prison. God showed Joseph the end, but failed to give him the details as to how he would step into his greatness.

Great people always have an experience to overcome and you are no different.

I do not consider myself a movie buff, but besides a good comedy, I love a movie whose main character defeats insurmountable odds. I love seeing a person who had a hard luck life, overcome it to become something powerful. I like those kinds of movies because it sends a message to all of us. The message it sends is that no matter how we start in life or what obstacles we are met with, we can overcome them. We are just like track runners. We are made to overcome our hurdles.

I have learned not to shy away from the detrimental things that have happened in my life. I have come to a place of understanding that my life is a storyline, not a mistake. Even the bad things have done more good than harm. Of course, when I was in the midst of my personal troubles, I thought the world was going to end. We always think that. We feel we are all alone. We think no one has experienced what we are experiencing. We think no one understands our pain, fears, and insecurities. All of us have a pit we have been pushed into or one we fell into. God trusts that once we are out of our pit, we will not be so quick to push somebody else into a pit and we will guide others in avoiding their pits. It is God's intent that your storyline becomes a movie for someone else. He sees you as an encourager; a person who can be just like Joseph when his dream was realized. Better, not bitter.

Joseph met his brothers again. He met them when he had been given a level of authority by Pharaoh. They feared he would retaliate against them for what they had done. He had every right to retaliate because his brothers had robbed him of years of life and relationship, especially with his father, Jacob. Joseph did not get even with his brothers nor did he blame them. He simply hugged them and said, "You meant evil against me; but God meant it for good" (Genesis 50:20). There are things that were set out to discourage, destroy, and dishonor you, but let it be used to deliver you. God is a scriptwriter and there is no greater script than the one that takes you up and not out. When God put you and I in the earth, He made us ready for the big screen of life. He wanted us to be a source of inspiration for anybody that wanted or needed to watch. I believe that Joseph's reaction was a great lesson for his family. If he could go through what he went through and receive his brothers with love in his heart, they had to take notice. They saw resilience not resentment. You too are resilient. You have staying power. You are a movie classic! I watch a good movie over and over and over again. You, my friend, are a good movie made for life. Pray with me:

Father, I thank You that You know all things. I thank You that You have made my life to be a blessing to someone else. Father, in the name of Jesus, help me to look at my life as a tool for others to use. Thank You for shielding me from some things and for what You have allowed me to experience. In Jesus name, amen.

19
A FRIEND OF GOD
God Sees You as a Friend

People always say I am a good friend. I do not know if that is totally accurate, but I would like to think I have learned how to be a good friend. I learned how to be a good friend by not being a good friend once. I will never forget it. I was a sixth grader at Highland Magnet School in Mrs. Chester's class. I do not remember all of the details, but all of my friends gave me the silent treatment because I repeated what one of them had told me. I cannot recall if it was detrimental or not, but being ignored felt terrible. I was only twelve years old at the time and I vowed from that moment on that I would never, ever repeat anything anybody tells me. That experience alone was instrumental in teaching me how to be confidential, a good listener, and how precious a true relationship is.

God wears a lot of hats in the lives of many of us. He is always revealing His many attributes and often we get to know Him in a entirely different light. For me, He has revealed Himself as Father, as Lord, and as Friend. Getting to know Him as Friend has been absolutely amazing, but more than that, His seeing me as a friend and my acceptance of that truth, is beyond my understanding. He wants you to know that He considers you a friend. One of my favorite worship songs is, "I Am a Friend of God," by

Israel Houghton. I get excited and grateful every time I hear the words:

> Who I am that You are mindful of me.
> That You hear me when I call.
> Is it true You are thinking of me
> How You love me, it's amazing.
>
> I am a friend of God
> I am a friend of God
> I am a friend of God
> He calls me friend.

Can you believe that God calls you His friend? What a powerful prophetic declaration from the very heart of God! It is especially powerful when you think of the bigness of God, His power and His strength. The best analogy I could make of this is to be best friends with the richest person in the world and have that person love you and treat you like you are the richest person in the world. Mindboggling! God looks at us as people He can share His most intimate thoughts with. Though I know He knows all things, I cannot begin to tell you the things I have shared with God. He knows my deepest secrets, yet I have not heard them again. He is my strongest confidante.

God says you are His friend. You can trust Him. You can whisper into His ear and it will not go any further than Him. Wow! Can you imagine that? It can be hard to believe if you have been betrayed by someone you trust. It is so easy to compare what God will do with what others have done to us. Looking back on the incident as a twelve year old, I do not know if I did what I was accused of, but the feeling of isolation was almost unbearable. That experience taught me what I should expect from a friend and how to be a friend to someone else. There are certain responsibilities I believe God holds Himself to because He sees you as a friend.

God can be trusted and He wants to trust you. You can tell Him anything and trust that His word is bond. It does not matter what you have done, you can trust Him with it. It can be the most vile, deepest, darkest thing any of us has ever done, yet you can trust Him. A real friend loves you no matter what. God is no different. We used to say that a real friend is there through "the thick and the thin." God is there with you when problems seem insurmountable. It is in those times, we feel alone and we feel like the whole world has gone on without us. God is still there and is well aware of where we are. He knows about every inch of our existence. Actually, the very hairs on our heads are numbered. He knows us to that degree. Even when we hurt Him or disappoint Him, He is still right there to love us.

The truth hurts. When God calls you friend sometimes that means He loves you enough to level with you. None of us like to be told the truth especially if it hurts. I have this one friend, Angie, who made a "living" making me mad because she made it her business to confront me with the truth. God is no different. He is constantly challenging us with the truth. His truth is meant to make us better, to build us to a greater dimension. None of us can become better if we refuse to hear the truth.

A true friend is often the biggest cheerleader. Whatever you endeavor to do, no one wants you to succeed more than God. In fact, it is He who gives us dreams, inspiration, and a innate desire to succeed. I have yet to meet anyone that wants to be on the bottom. Everyone wants to get to the top. God is cheering for you. He believes in you! He does not want any of us to fail. If you fall, He wants you to get back up and try again. He put inside of you a built-in mechanism called resilience. You were made not to quit. He made you to keep going. That is what faith is all about. Faith is not giving up when all odds are against you. The book of Hebrews (11:4-39) is filled with people that succeeded against the odds. We are from the same stock. We have all endured hard places. God cheers us on when we seem to be fading because He knows we got what it takes to keep pushing. One of my all-time favorite groups, The Impressions, recorded a song called, "We're a Winner." Curtis Mayfield sings, "We're a winner and never let anybody say boy, you can't make it 'cause a feeble mind is in your way. No more tears do we cry and we have finally dried our eyes and we're moving on up." What powerful words! Your enemy wants you to be defeated, but God says to you, "Win baby win!" I declare you are a winner. Pray with me:

Father, I thank You for being my friend and for seeing me as Yours. Help me to trust You even the more. Cause me to know that there is nothing going on in my life that is a surprise to You. You said the very hairs on my head are numbered, and I could cast every care upon You. Thank You for walking with me, believing in me, and always proving Yourself to me. Lord, I love you. Thank You for calling me friend. In the name of Jesus, I pray, amen.

20
FEAR NOT!
God Sees You as Fearless

It was a rainy, stormy Sunday afternoon, August 9, 1981. I sat in the living room, virtually in the dark, as my mother stood in the bathroom mirror fixing her hair. I could hear her clearly as she yelled to me, "You better not get up!" My nine year old heart pounded as the thunder crackled ferociously around me; the lightning lit up the room every few seconds. I just wanted to die! I wanted so desperately to move. I wanted to run and hide under my bed. I was too afraid of being struck by lightning. My heart roared for someone to rescue me. Not only was I still, I was frozen solid by dreadful fear.

I sat there because I had been afraid of bad weather all of my life and my mother thought by making me sit in the dark, in the midst of the storm, fear would be driven out of me. She thought I would eventually get used to storms and would not be afraid anymore.

Most of my life has been crippled by fear, particularly my childhood. If there was anything to be afraid of, I was: bands, dying, the dead, the dark, God, church "shouting," confrontation, and boys. Legend has it that when we were small, there was this terrible storm in Albany. It was so bad my mother ran into a closet with my twin sister and me running behind her. Somehow in the commotion of it all, I was momentarily left outside the door of the closet, hence my fear of bad weather. When we visited my maternal grandmother and there was a storm, we were told to be quiet because God was talking. I became too afraid to talk. Fear became a monster!

I wanted to talk about fear because it is one thing that can keep us from seeing ourselves as God sees us. Fear is so powerful that God emphatically declared in His Word that He did not give it to us. In 2 Timothy 1:7, the Apostle Paul told his spiritual son, Timothy, that God "has not given us a spirit of fear, but of power and of love and of a sound mind." For years, I thought fear had come from God until I realized He wanted me to be fearless. He wanted me to do what I never dreamed I could do.

Since I have been saved, I have constantly battled my own fears. Once, I went on a fast and after the fast, fear came into my bedroom. Yes! The spirit of fear paid me a visit with only one mission in mind, to make me more fearful. It came in the form of a man. He was fully dressed, but he had no head. When I rolled over and saw him, my heart tighten. I thought I was going to have a heart attack and die! God spoke to me. He said I had nothing to fear, for the head of fear was being cut off in my life.

Another time I was at home alone one night and there was a storm. I had a dream. In the dream I ran up and down the hallway scared out of my mind. As I ran, there was a big weight around my neck. Fear was undoubtedly a yoke in my life. It weighed me down; it kept me from doing a lot of things in my life.

Growing up, fear defined the perception I had of myself and my perception of God. I urge you not to let fear entangle you. Get to know yourself; get to know God- live, love, leap!

God has given you a lot of things, but fear is not one of them. If there is a boat, He wants you to get out of it. If there is ministry, He wants you to go to Nineveh. If there is a story, He wants you to write it. Whatever your fear, He wants you to overcome it! I urge you to confront your fears. Let fear know you will not be held hostage. It knows if it can hold you hostage, then it can take away your freedom. It wants to negate every single freedom you have in Christ. Adam and Eve hid from God because of fear and many of us are still hiding today. Why is fear hiding you from God? Fear does not want you to walk in power, express the love of God to others, or have a sound, stable mind. By giving us those three things, God is giving us tools of liberation. God does not want any of us to be bound by anything that would keep us from being an expression of who He is. This is what terrorism does. Fear is the greatest tool of terrorism. Terrorist groups use it because they know if they can get people afraid, they can make an entire nation stagnant. After thousands were killed in the deadliest terrorist attack in U.S. history on September 11, 2001, many were too afraid to get on an airplane.

In the same manner, spiritually, fear does not want you to fly. Fear does not want you to soar to new dimensions. It wants to keep you grounded, but God is calling you upward. Praise God! Let's pray:

Father, in Jesus' name, I declare Your name in the earth! You have not given me a spirit of fear, but You have given me power, love, and a sound mind. It is not Your will that I be afraid to take a risk. You have given me the ability to be Your expression in the earth and You are not afraid of anything. Father, deliver me from my fears. Give me boldness. Amen.

21
EPILOGUE: LEARNED BEHAVIOR

Seeing yourself as God sees you is learned behavior. You have to practice it daily, especially if you have been told all your life that you are nothing, a nobody, a loser. None of us came out of our mother's womb having it all together. When we exited the womb we entered not only a world filled with all kinds of problems, but people with problems.

I have never known anyone who did not have to overcome obstacles to reach success. All of us have had to endure heartache, and have experienced disappointment. We have to turn the negative that has been done to us into positive. We have to denounce all the bad behaviors we have learned. We have to be deprogrammed from our wrong thinking. Our minds have to be decoded. We have to treat our perception about God and His perspective of us like we treat a garden. I challenge you to only plant what is good for you. Do not plant seeds of doubt and fear. Tend the things of God. Water your faith in the Word of God. Uproot and weed out every negative thought and word spoken over you that goes against what God has said about you. Your garden needs sunlight to live, so hang around people who reinforce your value and are eager to push you into your God-given destiny. A lack of light will kill what you have planted.

Learned behavior is also a journey. If you have struggled with low self-esteem for years, you must commit yourself to discovering how powerful, important, and valuable you are. If you have spent a lifetime feeling unloved, you have to be willing to embark on the journey of being loved. It is like dating. You do not date someone one day and marry the person the very next day. You need time to get to know each other. In the same regard, you need time to get to know yourself and to know God, the Father. I challenge you to open your heart. Learning to see yourself as God sees you is a beautiful thing.

I encourage you to align yourself with the very thoughts of God. It is the thoughts and plans He has for us that will sustain us in trying times. Hold on to the dreams and aspirations He has given you. Whatever you do, keep pushing. Keep discovering every God-given gift and ability. There is no greater mission you can complete than the one God put inside you. What you have to offer is what the world has been waiting for, and your presence in the world is at the right time and the right place. I am glad you are here.

"The very time I thought I was lost, my dungeon shook and my chains fell off."

James Baldwin
The Fire Next Time

22
TOOLS YOU CAN USE

I pray that what I have shared with you has been beneficial to you. Regardless of what I have written, there is nothing more important than a personal relationship with God through Jesus Christ. My pastor, Bishop Victor L. Powell, has instilled some very important values in me. I wanted to share some of those tools with you:

1. You must live a life of prayer. If you want to see yourself as God sees you, you must spend time with God. Talk to Him. Let Him talk to you. He wants to commune with you. You do not have to give Him religious jargon, but you can speak from your heart. You can tell Him anything.

2. Spend time in the Word of God. I love the Word of God because I get to remind God of what He said about me. I also have to remind myself. Get in the Word and let it come alive in you. If you want to know all the things God promised you, you will find them in the Word of God.

3. Surround yourself with positive people. You deserve people that add to your life, not subtract

from it. The right people will always make it their business to encourage you, tell you the truth (even if it hurts), and stick with you through the thick and the thin.

4. You must have a stable voice in your life. I strongly encourage you have a pastor in your life that has the very heart of God. You need a pastor who spends time with God, reminds you of what God has said about you, and who pushes you into your destiny. I exhort you to find that voice for your life.

5. Make your life story available to others. There are many people who need to hear your story.

6. It is essential that you maximize all your God-given gifts and talents. All of us have a gift; therefore, share yours with others.

7. Cast all fears aside. All of us have been afraid to do something new, especially if no one else is doing it. Do not be afraid to be different. When you are daring to be different, you are, in essence, daring to be you.

8. Never forget where you have come from. Often we want to forget what we have been through, but there are things we may need to remember so we can learn from it, and teach others not to repeat it.

23
HARD QUESTIONS HARD ANSWERS

In seeing yourself as God sees you, I think there are several very important questions you need to ask yourself. Please take the time to reflect.

1. What do you think about yourself?

2. When you look at yourself in the mirror, what is the first thought that comes to your mind?

3. Reflect on the relationship you have (had) with your mother, father, or the person that raised you.

4. When you were growing up, were you afraid to meet new people? Or were you the center of attention?

5. If you tend to blame everybody else for your life, why do you blame everybody?

6. What were your greatest fears growing up?

7. What are your fears now?

8. What is your perspective of God?

9. If you have a difficult time accepting the love of others, why do you have a difficult time?

10. Do you believe that God loves YOU unconditionally? Why or why not?

11. What is the worst feeling you have ever felt?

12. If you are dealing with shame, express (if you can), what you feeling.

13. Do you have a difficult time forgiving yourself?

14. Is it difficult for you to accept God's forgiveness? If so, why?

15. Do you have a hard time forgiving others? If so, why?

16. How would you describe your life?

17. If you had to write a movie script about your life, what would you title it and why?

18. Do you have a mentor in your life? If so, why is that person your mentor?

19. How do you think God sees you?

20. In what ways have you been blessed by this book?

ABOUT THE AUTHOR

A native of Albany, GA, **Bummi Niyonu Anderson** is a writer, commentator, and author. Having written five other books, entitled, "Out of Darkness Into His Marvelous Light," "I Like it When: A Collection of Love Poems," "Love Lines: Poetry to Love," and "The Issues of Life." "You are A Masterpiece: Seeing Yourself as God Sees You" is her latest book.

Bummi has been writing for well over 20 years of her life. She has shared her poetry and commentary at readings on college campuses, at churches, cultural centers, and in poetry book compilations. Bummi has also been featured in *Charisma Magazine*, the world's largest Christian Magazine.

Bummi is a 1990 graduate of Dougherty Comprehensive High School and 1995 graduate of Albany State University, in Political Science. She is currently pursuing a Masters of Fine Art from National University.

Bummi is also an Associate Pastor at Rhema Word Cathedral in Albany, GA under the leadership of her spiritual father and mentor, Bishop Victor L. Powell.

Bummi resides in Albany, GA with her twin sister, Femi Nilaja, who is a graphic artist. They co-own Renaissance Connection and Double Xposure Media Group.

To order more copies of this book:

Go to: www.renaissanceconnect.com

or

www.amazon.com

You can follow Bummi on Twitter at:
@BumminNAnderson

Feel free to send your comments by
Connecting with Bummi on Facebook at

www.facebook.com/people/Bummi-Niyonu-Anderson

www.ingramcontent.com/pod-product-compliance
Lightning Source LLC
Chambersburg PA
CBHW060358050426
42449CB00009B/1787